CITYSCAPES

CITYS

JOHN KING

Heyday, Berkeley, California

CAPES

SAN FRANCISCO AND ITS BUILDINGS

Library of Congress Cataloging-in-Publication Data
King, John.
Cityscapes : San Francisco and Its buildings / John King.
    p. cm.
ISBN 978-1-59714-154-3 (pbk. : alk. paper)
1. Architecture—California—San Francisco. 2. San Francisco
(Calif.)—Buildings, structures, etc. I. Title. II. Title: San Francisco and Its buildings.
    NA735.S35.K56 2011
    720.9794'61—dc22
                2010046683

Cover photo: 353 Sacramento Street. Photo by John King.
Book design: Rebecca LeGates

Orders, inquiries, and correspondence should be addressed to:
        Heyday
        P.O. Box 9145, Berkeley, CA 94709
        (510) 549-3564, Fax (510) 549-1889
        www.heydaybooks.com

Printed in China by Print Plus Limited.

10 9 8 7 6 5 4 3 2 1

CONTENTS

To Cynthia Butler and Madeline King, for their wonderful perspectives and their eyes that see so much more than mine.

INTRODUCTION

Buildings in cities are remarkable things: they provide not only shelter but shared touchstones of reference and recall, shaping our sense of place as much as the skyline and the walls along the street. This is true of individual landmarks; it also is true of the overall composition, which, at its best, stands as mesmerizing and complex as a topographical form.

Certainly this is true of San Francisco, a city whose architectural abundance too often is taken for granted. Few structures aside from the Golden Gate Bridge are regarded as definitive works of this or that design school or era; rather, there's an assumption that because the whole is greater than the sum of the parts, the parts aren't all that important. This affectionate but condescending viewpoint even filters the perspective on such revered triumphs as the Ferry Building, made transcendent by its setting, and the Victorian-era homes with moldings and embellishments that often were ordered from catalogs.

Look closer, though, and you'll see that San Francisco's allure isn't a fluke of setting and climate, or the cumulative effect of people you encounter in cafés. It is a faceted tapestry that extends across neighborhoods, districts, and blocks. The new jostles the old, the tall frames the short, and the elaborate is made more striking by the proximity of the plain. The most luminous strands of the weave radiate a confidence that is neither meek nor glib. They share a sensibility more than a style, and they suit the city well.

That's why this book makes no claim to be a definitive roster of San Francisco's finest or most beloved works of architecture. Instead, look on it as fifty facets of our urban scene: the charismatic stars and the background players; buildings defined by bold visual moves and buildings that offer tactile delight; the sort of structure you notice every time you pass by, and the sort that escapes notice until you catch it at a certain angle, in a certain light. The focus is on specific works, but I hope that as a whole they convey something true to all great cities: that the landscape becomes more intriguing with the ongoing accumulation of layers.

To be sure, not everyone shares this view. The much-lauded "San Francisco values" stress tolerance and diversity, but they're laced with an architectural conservatism that would make Prince Charles beam. Many people who love "The City" look on tall buildings with fear and on contemporary design with scorn; they'd be content if the landscape were locked in place forever, starting with the day they arrived. I see things differently. The clash of styles and scales and materials can be invigorating—urban diversity at its best—so long as the new arrivals are marked by the essence of enduring architecture: begin with a clear vision and then bring it to life with loving care.

This book is an outgrowth of "Cityscape," a weekly column (too grand a label for a feature that consists of two or three photographs and fewer than one hundred words) that debuted in the *San Francisco Chronicle* in February of 2009. The prose has been revised and (slightly) expanded, and many of the photographs have not appeared before in print. I also have arranged the selections into four sections. "Icons" is self-evident, a handful of buildings that lodge themselves in civic memory. "Styles and Masters" explores the variety of architectures and architects within these city limits. "Landscape" is a primer on how to look at the built terrain around you. "Change" attempts to depict exactly that, from a variety of perspectives.

Some obvious treasures are missing—no City Hall, no Legion of Honor, no California Academy of Sciences or AT&T Park. But everything here shines in its own way as a distinctive piece in a much larger puzzle, one still taking form before our eyes.

Inevitably, a city such as San Francisco is defined in part by its most recognizable buildings—the ones with such presence that they seem more destined than designed.

Such structures serve as icons, and although that word in recent years has been slapped onto any sort of attention-seeking spectacle, it retains value nonetheless. Some buildings are icons by virtue of their architecture, while others conjure up historical or cultural associations. In either case, they say why this spot matters.

ICONS

Transamerica Pyramid

600 Montgomery Street

Reduced to its basics, there's little to love about the Transamerica Pyramid. It is concrete with a bit of quartz mixed in, topped by an aluminum cap, and punctured by 3,678 identical windows of no particular finesse. The shape is simple as well: diagonal and horizontal lines juxtaposed with two service-area "ears" protruding from the upper eighteen stories of the shaft. Yet it's a uniquely memorable building, a triumph of the unexpected, unreal and engaging all at once. That surprise is what locks the Pyramid in our public consciousness, decades after critics fought ardently to stop its construction. It is a presence and a persona, snapping into different focus with every fresh angle, every shift in light. *William L. Pereira and Associates, 48 stories, 1972*

Flood Building

870 Market Street

Some buildings dominate their surroundings if not the skyline, and there's no better example in San Francisco than the Flood Building— twelve stories of orderly pomp with a rounded prow that commands the corner of Powell and Market Streets with what a writer for *Architect and Engineer* in 1909 called "florid grandeur." Every detail is rooted and right, from the tall storefronts that beckon cable car daytrippers to the baroque cliff of the sandstone façade with its deep-chiseled windows and just enough ornamentation to enliven the mass rather than clutter the scene. You'd never guess this is a steel-frame building; it feels geomorphic, an outcrop on the terrain. *Albert Pissis, 12 stories, 1904*

Saint Anne of the Sunset

850 Judah Street

Religious buildings often serve not just as spiritual retreats but as neighborhood landmarks, symbols of home. Certainly that's the case with this Roman Catholic church and parish school that fills nearly a block of the Inner Sunset. Serene and magisterial at once, its twin towers and salmon hue and Romanesque-inspired rose window combine as an uplifting and immense counterpoint to the low-slung parade of single-family homes lining the streets around it. San Francisco has churches more architecturally distinct, more statuesque in their appearance or innovative in their design, but none has as far-reaching a presence, whether you're a believer or not. *Shea and Lofquist, 1931*

Contemporary Jewish Museum

736 Mission Street

There's rarely a spark when the present and past are joined in a single building, especially in a city as architecturally skittish as ours. That's why the Contemporary Jewish Museum is such electric fun: new spaces clad in brushed blue steel tumble from the masonry of an aged power station, Daniel Libeskind's update of what was conceived by the early-twentieth-century great Willis Polk. The brick walls adorned with white cherubs stand firm while the metal panels behind them shimmer bright one moment and go oily smooth the next. It's a compelling jostle, a magnetic hinge between Market Street and Yerba Buena Gardens that fuses old with new to bring out the best in both. *Willis Polk, 2008 update by Studio Daniel Libeskind with WRNS Studio, 2 stories, 1907*

Malloch Apartments
1360 Montgomery Street

For film buffs, one of San Francisco's most revered buildings is this suave perch on Telegraph Hill where Humphrey Bogart hid out with Lauren Bacall in the noir classic *Dark Passage:* five stories of curvaceous art moderne that slide toward the bay along the Filbert Steps. There's glass block in abundance, an open lobby with tropical airs, and a trio of silver murals that tattoo the white façade with scenes of Western exploration and innovation. The east slope of Telegraph Hill is now a fiercely protected historic district, mostly for the good, but playing defense in such a way also means we'll never again see something this seductive added to the scene. *Irvin Goldstine, murals by Alfred du Pont, 5 stories, 1937*

Conservatory of Flowers

John F. Kennedy Drive

If there's an architectural equivalent of a wedding cake, it's the Conservatory of Flowers in Golden Gate Park—a frosted concoction of wood and glass that seems unreal even as you step past lawns and palms into the billowing form. Millionaire James Lick ordered it in pieces from England only to let it languish on the grounds of his San Jose mansion. After his death, in 1876, the parts were sold by the estate to San Franciscans who assembled them on a terraced clearing near the park's eastern end, where it has presided ever since. A $25 million restoration completed in 2003 snuck in seismic bracing and freshened the Victorian frills, treating whimsy with the respect it deserves. *Assembled in 1879; 2003 restoration by Architectural Resources Group*

Lakeside Medical Center

2501 Ocean Avenue

Icons don't need to dominate a vista or pull out the stops; it's enough sometimes to strike a fond, familiar chord. Lakeside is a prim and manicured neighborhood in the city's distant west with a commercial center barely a block long, but it stands out by virtue of this streamlined exclamation point, a cross between a tower and a marquee that pops from a two-story medical office otherwise cloaked in colonial garb. Add that the tower marks the narrow end of a triangular block with a light-rail stop across the way, and we have the architectural equivalent of a map's You Are Here marker—a simple but memorable landmark, retro and relevant all at once. *Harold Stoner, 2 stories, 1941*

City Lights Bookstore

261 Columbus Avenue

Everyone knows City Lights, a fermenter of intellectual mischief since 1953 so integral to San Francisco's cultural landscape that in 2001 the Board of Supervisors proclaimed it Landmark No. 228 as a tribute to its "association with major developments in post–World War II literature as publisher of Beat Generation writers." But the bookstore's aged home also tells an architectural tale. There's no flash or affectation, just tall wood-trimmed windows that let the books set the mood beneath arched masonry openings. It is a frame to be filled by whatever the future might bring and, in the process, it endures with sturdy ease. *Oliver Everett, 2 stories, 1907*

San Francisco Federal Building
90 Seventh Street

Startling structures often become less so with time, but the San Francisco Federal Building still sticks in many a craw. No wonder: too much concrete confronts visitors, and the view from the south presents a 115-foot-wide slab draped in perforated steel panels that juts up and over the eighteen-story wall, as if it were some clattering metallic beast. And yet. There's adventure in the careen of shadows and forms, the eleventh floor's through-building terrace, and the proud display of sustainability. (The long slab allows natural light and air to circulate, for instance.) If this building is easier to respect than to love, it deserves our attention nonetheless. *Morphosis with SmithGroup, 18 stories, 2007*

2500 Steiner Street

What a shock *this* must have caused when it rose in the Roaring Twenties—twelve tall stories and a red-tile peak, easily four times the height of any of the mansions it joined on the edge of Alta Plaza Park in Pacific Heights. And consider the impudent nonchalance of a decorous Mission-flavored coat on a modern steel frame. Yet now 2500 Steiner looks thoroughly at home, assured but urbane, the smooth ascent of its white plaster walls culminating in that masonry crown. The only embroidery is at ground level, where terra-cotta moldings wrap the entrance in a baked Gothic veneer. Were all towers this elegant, the new ones wouldn't stir such a fuss. *C. A. Meussdorffer, 12 stories, 1926*

SHELL BUILDING

Shell Building
100 Bush Street

A great skyscraper excels up close as well as from afar, delivering tactile pleasures with the skyline rush. The Shell Building does both, and more. The compact silhouette of the shaft—capped by a cornice with emphatic castings of shells, of course—takes cues from Eliel Saarinen's acclaimed but unbuilt design for the Chicago Tribune Tower competition of 1922. This stylish tower by George Kelham (whose Russ Building of the same era casts a similar spell) shimmers even more on the ground, where deep-ridged panels of glazed terra-cotta have a sandy glow that captures shadows and attracts your glance, then your touch. *George Kelham, 28 stories, 1929*

Sentinel Building

916 Kearny Street

Say what you want about ostentatious wealth, hubris can be a boon to the public realm. It was early-twentieth-century political boss Abe Ruef who erected this sliver-thin riot of copper bays and a ceremonial dome to use as his base of operations (until he was found guilty of graft in December of 1908, that is). After a 1958 upgrade defied the era's wrecking balls and the Kingston Trio briefly held the deed, enter Francis Ford Coppola, of *Godfather* fame—who poured another fortune into restoring the copper's weathered green patina while converting the ground floor into an amply windowed restaurant. Let the Pyramid loom; for true San Franciscans, the Sentinel will suffice. *Salfield and Kohlberg, 1958 restoration by Henrik Bull, 8 stories, 1906*

As the layers of a city accumulate, so do the architectural lessons to be learned. Styles first seen as dull gain a sense of decorum; flash can fade to acceptable fun. Hindsight allows judgment after the shock of the new wears off.

San Francisco shows this well, since so much of the past remains and the most important feature—the terrain—frames everything else. In a few happy cases, it also has prodded some of the world's finest architects to do some of their finest work.

STYLES and MASTERS

Sharon Building

Martin Luther King and Bowling Green Drives

No nineteenth-century American architect had more influence than Henry Hobson Richardson, whose landmarks, including Chicago's Glessner House and Trinity Church in Boston, are so powerful that his name came to define a style in itself. The closest thing the Bay Area has to a bona fide Richardson is the quadrangle of Stanford University, designed by his firm after the founder's death, in 1886. But San Francisco *does* have a spirited pastiche alongside the playground at Golden Gate Park—the Sharon Building, with its sandstone-block walls, squat columns, broad arches, and ceremonial brawn. Even children who never attend the craft workshops inside learn a lesson about the arts: Architecture can be an emotional force. *Percy and Hamilton, 3 stories, 1887*

1660 Haight Street

San Francisco has few built examples of Art Nouveau, a theatrical
style associated with fin-de-siècle Paris in which the ornamentation
is the show, so how fitting it is that the trippiest survivor resides on
ever-theatrical Haight Street. The lurid red paint job is recent and so
is the wizened infant at the peak of the cornice. But most of the other
embellishments date to when this building debuted as a nickelodeon,
which gave way to a conventional movie house, then a neighborhood
market, and now a clothing bazaar that's an ideal fit. Local fashions
change, and local needs as well; Haight Street, one warrants, will remain
over-the-top for some time to come. *Bernard J. Joseph, 2 stories, 1911*

1–7 Russian Hill Place

Willis Polk is best remembered for his Pacific Heights mansions and the precedent-setting glass curtain wall of 1917's Hallidie Building at 150 Sutter Street, but his most adroit tribute to San Francisco is this quartet of linked homes atop Russian Hill. The western slope is held in place by a retaining wall complete with regal balustrade; at the top the scale turns cloistered as what seems to be a row of cottages with dark wood bays lines a brick alley that ends, incongruously, at a twenty-six-story residential tower from the 1960s. No matter. Polk's ensemble feels wholly of its time and fully at home in ours—and truly, it would make sense nowhere else. *Willis Polk, 2 stories, 1916*

Leonard R. Flynn
Elementary School

3125 Cesar Chavez Street

This school on the Bernal Heights edge of the Mission District was designed by John Galen Howard, the architect responsible for many UC Berkeley treasures, and it embodies the classic ideal of education as something imparted from above, all formal order and time-honored rules. Since 1977 it has conveyed an additional message, for the south wall serves as the canvas for an incandescent wall mural, the art form that has become the Mission's defining visual trait. The juxtaposition doesn't mar Howard's temple of learning: it's a vivid affirmation of community, and a demonstration of the ease with which confident buildings can absorb cultural change. *John Galen Howard, 1977 mural conceived by Susan Cervantes of Precita Eyes, 3 stories, 1924*

400 Castenada Avenue

Forest Hill is the sort of neighborhood where Mission Revival nods to Mock Tudor across hillside paths that are announced with Grecian urns and lead from one artfully meandering roadway to the next. Adding to the genteel ambiance: such delights as this cross between a storybook cottage and a baronial estate. What should be saccharine pretense instead cloaks itself with wooden gables, slate-clad rooflines, leaded glass and—the head-turner—walls of limestone rubble. This is make-believe of the best sort, a reminder that historical styles are best when delivered not in a dutiful tone but with genuine craft and a spirited twist. *Harold Stoner, 2 stories, 1927*

Roosevelt Middle School

460 Arguello Boulevard

Timothy Pflueger is revered in San Francisco for such Jazz Age showpieces as 450 Sutter Street and the City Club. Don't look for Art Deco at his Roosevelt Middle School in the Inner Richmond, though. This is 1920s modernism with an industrial European bent, a three-story block that comes alive in the snap of copper-framed windows amid chiseled brickwork, or the battlement-like accents beneath a tower of propulsive thrust. Throughout his career, Pflueger understood instinctively that a city's most resonant buildings are the ones that strike a visceral chord, no matter what their style might be. *Miller and Pflueger, 3 stories, 1930*

140 Maiden Lane

San Francisco's had mixed luck with buildings by architectural Big Names, but an unquestioned triumph resides on narrow Maiden Lane. Not only is it the city's one structure by the biggest Big Name of all, Frank Lloyd Wright, this former V. C. Morris Gift Shop combines the intricate craft of Wright's early work with the kinetic spark of his later years. The passerby sees a tan cliff with brickwork distinctive enough to make it intriguing rather than inert, and then the deep scoop of a portal pulls you into a ramped retail space that predates the better-known Guggenheim by a decade. Wright's design walls off the street, an urban sin. But for great architects on a roll, the rules don't apply. *Frank Lloyd Wright, 2 stories, 1949*

Russell House

3778 Washington Street

German architect Eric Mendelsohn earned the favor of his peers in the 1920s for buildings that softened the continent's modernist rigor with ebullient curves. When the Nazis took power he moved to England and then Palestine before settling in San Francisco after World War II, where he lived until his death in 1953. The lone house he designed here is a classic, with three stories of redwood-clad right angles shrouded in green and then, at the northwest corner, a swirl of balconied grace that seems to defy gravity. Outsiders sometime grasp the attributes of a place more clearly than do locals, and this is The City distilled to its essence: drama and views. *Eric Mendelsohn, 3 stories, 1950*

675 California Street

Architectural historian Vincent Scully once likened the essence of International Style modernism to "an uncomplicated intellectual order." The best local example, oddly enough, is tucked against the edge of Chinatown across from 1853's Old St. Mary's Church. A clean jewel of steel and glass softened by the trees of St. Mary's Square, the narrow three-story box looks less like a building than a pristine diagram that happens to be displayed amid battered masonry and happily dissonant cable cars. An especially deft touch is the circular staircase; placed in the most visible corner, it makes the interior life of the building part of the overall design. *A. E. Waegeman, 3 stories, 1964*

450 Sansome Street

Let's be honest: 450 Sansome embodies everything wrong with 1960s architecture. It's a dull block of Anywhere USA that plants a row of columns along the sidewalk and continues them upward sixteen stories to a flat finale (shoebox without end, amen). But one change did wonders for the street-level ambiance: the 2007 addition of a scalloped ground-level foyer of aqua-green glass topped by an aluminum canopy resting on lithe diagonal struts. The sleek fishbowl with its retail space and lobby entrance does more than add a twenty-first-century twist. It nudges you to notice long-ignored grace notes in the tower, like the embossed metal panels that gleam in the sun. *Richard Hadley, 2007 addition by Mark Dzlewulski, 16 stories, 1965*

Glen Park BART Station

2901 Diamond Street

With a name like Brutalism, no wonder the public never warmed to this raw strain of architecture that arrived in America from Europe in the 1960s. Yet the movement produced such evocative works as Glen Park's BART station, where the shadowy drama comes from the interplay of heavy forms, one pushing past the next. The boxy exterior with its drab plaza gives no hint of what's below: tucked deep inside the earth, under a raised muscular shell, trains rush in and out through a brooding grandeur of rough concrete against polished stone, blunt structural beams, and sharp shafts of light. BART has forty-three stations; this surely is the best. *Ernest Born with Corlett and Spackman, below ground, 1973*

353 Sacramento Street

Some buildings gain appeal in the rearview mirror, when you can be sure they don't signal some disturbing new trend. This metal building with an aquamarine tint is vintage 1970s corporate modernism, high-tech and thin-skinned, gleaming slick as ice amid buildings clad in concrete, brick, and stone. Though the contrast remains jarring, the abstract purity of the design wears well—there's a hint of I. M. Pei in the tower's diagonal cut—and it serves as a smooth chaser to the earthy neighbors. Different yet demure, modest in scale, this tower knows its place. All good buildings reflect that wisdom, though it might take time to become apparent. *Skidmore, Owings and Merrill, 23 stories, 1982*

101 California Street

Skyscrapers are fueled by ego, the quest to pierce the heavens with strong simple strokes, and 101 California shows you don't need a romantic profile to announce you've arrived. This six-hundred-foot tower was conceived by notorious style-hopper Philip Johnson as a saw-toothed barrel that narrows slightly as it rises, vertical notches of granite and glass accentuating the height. This isn't a masterpiece; the plaza serves as a launching pad, and any stray human is a mere dot against oversized walls and a thicket of columns, as though New York's marquee architect lacked interest in anything except skyline oomph. But what oomph! I only wish it soared another one hundred feet, chilled glamour all the way. *Johnson/Burgee Architects, 48 stories, 1982*

2910 California Street

Here's another case where San Francisco is enriched by a well-done exception to the rules—specifically, the rules of neighborhood context and urban design. Instead of lining up straight along the street, five playfully compressed cottages telescope into a settled block of Pacific Heights, a cleaved fissure in what otherwise is a static urban scene. The jolt is underscored by the city's most nuanced example of Postmodern design—an architectural movement in vogue during the 1980s that evoked the past with wry humor and a certain detachment. If the majority of "PoMo" now looks dated and glib, this slice avoided that trap. It substitutes intelligent fun for predictable kitsch, lacing style with substance. *Kotas/Pantaleoni Architects, 3 stories, 1989*

M. H. de Young Memorial Museum

50 Hagiwara Tea Garden Drive

Truly gifted architects go beyond building design to unlock the world around us. Switzerland's Jacques Herzog and Pierre de Meuron did this at Golden Gate Park, where no local architect would have conceived anything as audacious as an observation tower atop the reborn de Young Museum (or, if they had, they would have kept silent for fear of public catcalls). But the pair presented this as the logical conclusion to a civic museum in such a forested setting, and now there's a glassed-in pavilion 130 feet in the air. The museum itself is supple, with a dour but exotic copper skin; the tower is a revelation, literally adding a new dimension to a city we thought we knew. *Herzog and de Meuron with Fong and Chan Architects, 2 stories plus 144-foot tower, 2005*

As important as singular landmarks might be, the weave of a city is what lingers in the mind. The cumulative character of the buildings and spaces you encounter along the way is every bit as important as what you set out to find.

And the more you know a city, the truer this becomes. San Francisco is blessed with buildings that offer life-sized lessons in place-making. They're imbued with a feel for proportions and craft, and they aren't afraid to put on a show.

LANDSCAPE

Flatiron Building

540 Market Street

The architectural landscape of San Francisco is enhanced by infinite variations on a theme, where districts dominated by older buildings never grow cloying because no two structures are quite the same. Here's a great example from 1913 that, at eleven stories, was tall for its time. Most of the way up it's glassy and gaunt, atmospheric but not distinct—until the sunlight directs attention to the cornice, a splashy parade of Gothic embroidery that marches well beyond the outer walls. The conclusion is so exuberant you wonder if the designers planned it that way, or if the construction crew received the topping to a more grandiose building by mistake. *Havens and Toepke, 11 stories, 1913*

77 New Montgomery Street

The unexpected takes a different form down the block and around the corner, where a broad two-story box from 1907 grew by three floors in 1920. The basic lines are nothing special—a rectangular frame punctured by rectangular windows—and the decorated sheet-metal cornice has none of the Flatiron's verve, but those upper three floors offer a unique staccato charge. Each window is outlined by a zipper of white bricks stacked back and forth, in and out. The architectural term is "dentilation"; the effect is a syncopated dance skimming an otherwise plain surface, the sort of wonderful touch that no architect would think of today. *Sylvan Schnaittacher, 1920 addition by Mel I. Schwartz, 5 stories, 1907*

91 Central Street

The virtues of infinite variation are most apparent in older residential
neighborhoods defined by Victoriana of a nature ebullient and
idiosyncratic enough, again and again, to catch you off guard. Downhill
from Buena Vista Park, this eight-unit apartment building starts simple
with three stories smack against the sidewalk in the middle of a dense
block. The fun comes in the joyous amplification. The classical columns
are oversized; medallion-like flourishes look as though they were
ordered from Pompeii; the lacquered paint pretends that it's marble.
Only a stickler would say the details tip toward excess, for the generosity
of spirit is what lingers in your mind. *James Francis Dunn, 3 stories, 1904*

Pacific Primary School

1501 Grove Street

"Form follows function" is the modernist creed, but color can signal function as well; the simple shapes and bright tones of this preschool strike a playful chord that any pupil would find inviting. Meanwhile, grown-ups can discern sophisticated architecture in the patterned depth as sections of the façade overlap with a clarity that complements nearby Victorians even as the new building employs horizontal forms rather than vertical bays. The entrance is tucked beneath the action, accented by one deep cut and warmed to human scale by resin-impregnated panels of recycled wood. As for the bike racks shaped like real bicycles…once you start being playful, why not go all the way?

Tom Eliot Fisch, 2 stories, 2008

Alexis Apartments

380–390 Clementina Street

Color goes only so far—it can't make a squat building soar, or turn flat stucco into carved stone—but a fresh coat of paint can bring latent rhythms to life. When the Alexis Apartments stood along Fifth Street wearing a coat of tombstone gray (runner-up to beige as the default hue of too many local structures), its fourteen-story slabs sent the message that in this part of town, appearances don't matter. Then the senior housing got a makeover, announced with a pastel paint scheme to step up what architectural drama exists while adding liveliness to the scene. Now these background towers hint at the energy around them; Piet Mondrian would approve. *John Minton, 2009 renovation by Barcelon and Jang, 14 stories, 1972*

101 Howard Street

The low rake of winter sun flatters older structures clad in rough stone and hand-placed brick, sharpening the lines flattened by fog or bright skies. This National Register landmark began life as the offices and roastery of Folgers Coffee Co., riding out the 1906 earthquake on wooden piles driven forty feet into the bay fill below. At any hour of the day, these deep three-story arches with their New Orleans–ornate balconies have a character that can't be mimicked by stucco or precast panels. But in a certain light close by dawn or dusk, magic takes hold of buildings like this. Everything new fades into the background, whatever its size might be. *Henry Schulze, 5 stories, 1904*

Adam Grant Building

114 Sansome Street

It's a good rule of thumb in San Francisco to take what you see with a grain of salt. Consider this stately brick concoction from 1908, with such classical adornments as a stony garland above the entrance and urns at the twelfth-floor corners. In fact, the original garland vanished in a misbegotten 1960s modernization and the original urns were removed around the same time for seismic reasons, since the landlords were not willing to spend the money to anchor them in place. But in 2000, a new owner took advantage of the dot-com boom to restore lost frills, including fiberglass replicas of the garland and urns. That's how a city holds its luster: when times are good, people lavish it with care. *Howard and Galloway, 2000 restoration by Ottolini Booth and Associates, 14 stories, 1908*

Maskey Building

48 Kearny Street

The sleight-of-hand on downtown streets goes beyond the occasional fiberglass frill. As evidence, consider this sparkling white façade that hides a bold white lie. The embellished terra-cotta went up in 1908 as part of the Maskey Building, a collection of offices above shops, but seventy-five years later the site was folded into a high-rise project next door and the Maskey was demolished. Almost. Four bays of the façade were moved down the block, to line up with Maiden Lane, and then restored, fire escapes and all, to mask a low wing of the new tower. Which makes the Maskey nothing more than an atmospheric trinket—one displayed with such pride you can't help but cherish the ruse.

Havens and Toepke, 6 stories, 1908

Heineman Building

130 Bush Street

Measuring just twenty feet wide and ten stories high, pressed tight by larger rivals, this building began life after the 1906 earthquake as a necktie, belt, and suspender factory. Logically it should disappear into the masonry forest of the old Financial District; instead, the architects made every thin inch count by running a Gothic bay up the façade so that vertical lines of creamy terra-cotta streak past hammered copper spandrels and conclude with spires that would look thoroughly at home in medieval France. An inspired riff more than a sustained composition, this compressed delight shows how, in the right hands, the most unpromising site can shine. *MacDonald and Applegarth, 10 stories, 1910*

Hugo Building

200 Sixth Street

No affection was lavished on the Hugo building, a residential hotel that festered empty for twenty years until the city was able to buy it in 2009 using the power of eminent domain. What sets the Hugo apart from other scabs of skid row blight is Brian Goggin's "Defenestration," an installation added in 1997 that features salvaged furniture seeming to tumble from windows, held back by neither gravity nor fear. "Defenestration" will remain until demolition occurs—new housing for low-income residents is in the works—but let us remember what this corner says about public art: earnest civic messages are no match for imaginative work that makes us rear back and then smile. *Theo W. Lenzen, 1997 artwork by Brian Goggin, 4 stories, 1909*

101 Second Street

"Civility" isn't a word found in architecture dictionaries, but it defines this glassy tower that signaled the new century's shift of the skyline to the south. Though tall, 101 Second steps upward from the Second and Mission corner with moves comprehended easily on the ground; though unapologetically modern, the pale limestone and punched windows on sections of the façade fall in line with older neighbors. Finally, the glass walls at the corner enclose a sixty-foot-high "art pavilion" open to all. City planners since 1985 have required downtown projects to include public space; no other example is so enticing, or so integral to the neighboring scene. *Skidmore, Owings and Merrill, 26 stories, 1999*

Like it or not, change shapes our surroundings. Even if heights are tamped down and certain looks are enforced, cultures alter their environments in ways that can't be planned. Neighborhood life brings new expectations, blocks turn hot or cold, each generation defines urban life anew.

Buildings bear witness to this and allow us, in turn, to use them to gauge the marks of time. A varied cityscape is part of a much larger story, the core of which is that San Francisco and other large cities are in a state of constant flux. This is something we should savor, not resent or ignore.

CHANGE

Harrigan Weidenmuller Building

344 Kearny Street

Each building is a work of architecture, and a lens that lets us view how, in cities, time never stands stills. The Baroque flourishes on this glassy cube were designed to project a sense of commercial permanence back in 1927, and indeed the real estate leasing firm Harrigan Weidenmuller still operates from offices nearby. But the oh-so-carefully composed frame of the firm's former home now houses the most transitory of retail operations—a nail salon—with a clientele that draws heavily from nearby Chinatown. Look above the cornice for another sign of the age: a cheerful shot of graffiti that suggests even humble Kearny Street has its artistic passersby. *Architect unknown, 1 story, 1927*

1019 Market Street

Architectural overstatement can also be a virtue when you bid for attention in the middle of a block and stand your ground with aplomb. The Eastern Outfitting Co. department store that built this is long gone, as is the notion of Market Street as a place where families might shop. What remains above the boarded storefront is the monumentality of a single, broad five-story bay framed by ceremonial Corinthian columns, the workaday brick of the side walls on view just inches away. This wonder of self-promotion maintains its dignity on a grim stretch of Market that city officials and feuding activists have let decay. Someday, perhaps, it will have the neighbors and neighborhood it deserves. *George A. Applegarth, 6 stories, 1909*

353 Folsom Street

This rugged chunk of blue-collar heft—a copper foundry into the 1960s, mostly architect offices since then—is the antithesis of everything that has sprouted of late on Rincon Hill. Instead of craning skyward for views it hunkers low to the ground; the walls are thick concrete rather than thin glass, and the crisp black window mullions are the only hint that there's been a thorough restoration inside. By its atmospheric presence, the former foundry offers a measure of how the surroundings have evolved, in usage as well as scale—which is one of the best arguments for saving the truest buildings from different eras, no matter how humble they might be. *Architect unknown, 2 stories, 1920s*

1098 Valencia Street

Aside from funeral parlors, the most distinguished buildings in older neighborhoods often are older banks, where classical details were used to convey an air of financial calm. This orderly gem was designed for Hibernia Bank by Arthur Brown, Jr. (of City Hall renown), one of several he did for the institution, and it's an unexpected sight on today's Valencia Street. The Irish families of the Mission District that banked here gave way to Latino families long ago; the pharmacy across the street is a hipster diner, and there's an avant-garde theater down the block. But the patriarch remains an arched stone anchor, one that shrugs off all social tides. *Bakewell and Brown, 3 stories, 1924*

Agriculture Building

101 The Embarcadero

This masonry outpost on the Embarcadero began life as a post office, tight against the water so mail-laden ferries could pull right up to the wide-open back. Now it offers a perspective on the evolution of architecture and the city. We gauge the waterfront's shift from working port to pleasure ground as well as the lost glories of a world where functional buildings aspired to a tone of ornate awe. It's also a horizontal footstool to the vertical ascension of a downtown in which sky-high budgets nonetheless frown on the playfulness of burnt-yellow blocks of terra-cotta that long to be marble, or painted iron griffins above the door. *A. A. Pyle, 2 stories, 1915*

Pacific Telephone Building

140 New Montgomery Street

The Pacific Telephone Building long towered over the South of Market neighborhood as a lone promontory on the other side of the tracks, sheer majesty slightly out of place. The city's center of gravity has shifted so that taller towers now crowd near, with more to come, but this Roaring Twenties triumph remains the one that stands out. The white walls of glazed terra-cotta charge upward, each flourish unfurled with glee, and no L-shaped slab ever looked so potent. Even sitting empty—a restoration as housing is planned—the shaft glows. If there's a moral, it's that height goes only so far; the true peaks of our skyline are measured by passion and verve. *Miller and Pflueger with A. A. Cantin, 26 stories, 1925*

Palace Garage

125 Stevenson Street

A good service building signals its presence with moves that don't make a lot of fuss but at the same time can't be mistaken for anything else. That's the case with this worn but urbane bit of 1920s class tucked down an alley across from the Palace Hotel. One neon sign tells you that it's a garage and two neon arrows above over-scaled portals point drivers the way in and out. As obvious as this sounds, the framed openings add dignity, and the neon, radiant grace. As for the weary gray façade, consider it part of the old-school ambiance. Sam Spade could be loitering outside at dusk and he'd thoroughly blend into the scene.

O'Brien Brothers, 4 levels, 1921

Downtown Center Garage

325 Mason Street

No decorative stonework masks this nine-story spiral of concrete that opened in 1954 to make life easier for suburbanites wanting to visit Union Square's theaters and shops. Instead we have the city's purest example of function-fueled form. The ramp for traffic circulation is treated as a sculptural object, a compact tilt of angled lines that skim past circular columns pulled back so as not to mar the razor-thin first impression. In today's San Francisco, where cars are scorned if not banned, this unapologetic ode to automotive convenience is as archaic as a log cabin—and a relic of efficient beauty, if you give it half a chance.

George A. Applegarth, 9 levels, 1954

450 South Street

This garage from 2009 takes the balance between function and decoration to the other extreme: it is a punctured canvas, an abstraction of angled solids and deep voids that slides as the sun shifts across the façade's pearly stucco. These forms don't need neon to catch the eye—the contrast to the office-park-like neighbors is enough—but they're emphasized by the concrete staircase at one corner that locks the composition into the earth, while a recessed glass fence along the sidewalk pays respect to human scale. No matter what bicycle advocates wish, cars are part of our lives. This garage, like the two preceding examples, makes a virtue of necessity. *WRNS Studio, 7 levels, 2009*

Kayak House

Mission Creek Park

Infrastructure takes all forms in the twenty-first century, including such once-exotic tasks as keeping kayaks safe and dry, and this storage hut near the west end of Mission Creek is the most lyrical shed you'll ever see. Imagine a graceful tent open at both ends, the long sides arcing up and in until the ribs slide past each other, tepee-like, one side cloaked in translucent blue plastic and the other in stained wooden slats. Nestled beneath the thrumming sweep of Interstate 280 near a mundane chunk of master-planned Mission Bay, blissfully dismissive of the drear and noise, there's no big message here save one: Whatever is worth doing is worth doing well. *MKThink, 28 feet tall, 2008*

Mission Creek Houseboats

300 Channel Street

The stylistic opposite of the kayak shed—and everything else nearby—are the twenty "floating homes" along Mission Creek. The community has existed in one ramshackle form or another since the 1950s, when freight trains were the only neighbors. No longer: the north side of Mission Creek is lined with luxury housing, and a UCSF campus is rising to the south. The floating colony has a lease until 2055, so the homes will remain as happy iconoclasts, each one quirkier than the next. In today's city with its dour watchdogs and discriminatory prices, the challenge is finding space for *new* communities like this to take hold—the ones nobody can plan, the ones we could never predict.

Spire

North of Arguello Gate, off of Arguello Boulevard

Not a building per se, but a structure nonetheless. This steep pyramid in
a clearing near the Presidio's Arguello Gate takes thirty-seven cypresses
felled as part of the park's ongoing reforestation and bundles them
with statuesque care, lodged in concrete and linked by hidden bolts.
The rigid collage seems out of place, except that its materiality is the
materiality of a forest itself imposed by man, in a former military base
that now serves as a national park. As for those knee-high saplings
surrounding the spike, with time they'll grow nearly as tall, one
intervention absorbing the next. English environmental artist Andy
Goldsworthy probably didn't intend an organic analogy to our ongoing
urban transformations, but here it is. Some change is obvious the
moment it occurs. Other change—often the most significant—escapes
our notice unless we know how to look. *Andy Goldsworthy, 90 feet tall, 2008*

ACKNOWLEDGMENTS

Like much of what appears in newspapers, the *San Francisco Chronicle* column that spawned this book came about by chance. I'd been mulling over ways to convey in print the episodic nature of the city landscape when—serendipity—Editor Ward Bushee asked if there were some fresh way, in words and imagery, to tap into the palpable affection that San Franciscans feel for their surroundings. And "Cityscape" was born.

So I want to start by thanking Ward for the initial nudge. But newspapers are collaborative efforts, and I've been blessed with coworkers who share my enthusiasm for the Bay Area's urban fabric (though they wouldn't use such a highfalutin phrase). Managing Editor Stephen Proctor and former City Editor Kenneth Conner carved space for architecture in an era of shrinking resources. Editors Audrey Cooper, Kristen Go, and David Lewis keep me focused on writing for regular people rather than trained architects. In the Photography department, Kathleen Hennessy put a camera in my hands, saying I best knew the building details to stress, while Dan Jung critiqued my early shots with candor leavened by wit. Both have left the paper, and both are missed. At Heyday, it was George Young's idea that a procession of squibs might add up to a book. Gayle Wattawa has focused the mix and Lisa K. Manwill has sharpened the prose. And long before a book was ever in the cards, Allan Temko and Marty F. Nolan showed me how much fun the act of writing about a city can be.

Work of this sort also relies—immensely—on getting the facts and getting them right. Lucky for me, many San Franciscans not only love old buildings but make it their business to know who did what, when. Two people in particular have bailed me out time and again: N. Moses Corrette of the San Francisco's Department of City Planning, and Christopher VerPlanck of Knapp and Verplanck Preservation Architects.

Finally, a word about the title.

When Ken Conner told me he planned to name the column "Cityscape" I balked, noting that *Boston Globe* architecture critic Robert Campbell used that name for his column in the 1980s. To which Ken responded, "So?" Off went an apologetic email to Robert, who shrugged that an editor had named *his* column as well, despite Robert's protestation that "Cityscape" was then in use by the *Washington Post*'s first architecture critic, Wolf von Eckardt. Once my column debuted I received my own heads-up, from Blair Kamin of the *Chicago Tribune*. Editors were giving his column "The Skyline" a new moniker: "Cityscapes."

All of which suggests that architectural criticism is like architecture itself: a few basic ideas handed back and forth. Me, I'm lucky to be in such company.

ABOUT THE AUTHOR

John King is the *San Francisco Chronicle*'s Urban Design Critic. He joined the paper in 1992 and has been in his current post since 2001. His work has been honored by groups including the California Preservation Foundation, the Society of Professional Journalists, and the California chapters of the American Institute of Architects and the American Planning Association, and he is a two-time finalist for the Pulitzer Prize in Criticism. An honorary member of the American Society of Landscape Architects, he was also the recipient in 2006 of the first Gene Burd Award for Urban Journalism, presented by the Urban Communication Foundation. He lives in Berkeley with his wife and daughter.

HEYDAY
into California

About Heyday

Heyday is an independent, nonprofit publisher and unique cultural institution. We promote widespread awareness and celebration of California's many cultures, landscapes, and boundary-breaking ideas. Through our well-crafted books, public events, and innovative outreach programs we are building a vibrant community of readers, writers, and thinkers.

Thank You

It takes the collective effort of many to create a thriving literary culture. We are thankful to all the thoughtful people we have the privilege to engage with. Cheers to our writers, artists, editors, storytellers, designers, printers, bookstores, critics, cultural organizations, readers, and book lovers everywhere!

We are especially grateful for the generous funding we've received for our publications and programs during the past year from foundations and hundreds of individual donors. Major supporters include:

Anonymous; Audubon California; Barona Band of Mission Indians; B.C.W. Trust III; S. D. Bechtel, Jr. Foundation; Barbara and Fred Berensmeier; Berkeley Civic Arts Program and Civic Arts Commission; Joan Berman; Peter and Mimi Buckley; Lewis and Sheana Butler; Butler Koshland Fund; California Council for the Humanities; California Indian Heritage Center Foundation; California State Coastal Conservancy; California State Library; California Wildlife Foundation / California Oak Foundation; Keith Campbell Foundation; John and Nancy Cassidy Family Foundation, through Silicon Valley Community Foundation; Christensen Fund; Compton Foundation; Creative Work Fund; Lawrence Crooks; Nik Dehejia; Donald and Janice Elliott, in honor of David Elliott, through Silicon Valley Community Foundation; Evergreen Foundation; Federated Indians of Graton Rancheria; Mark and Tracy Ferron; Furthur Foundation; George Gamble; The Fred Gellert Family Foundation; Wallace Alexander Gerbode Foundation; Richard & Rhoda Goldman Fund; Wanda Lee Graves and Stephen Duscha; Evelyn & Walter Haas, Jr. Fund; Walter & Elise Haas Fund; James and Coke Hallowell; Sandra and Chuck Hobson; James Irvine Foundation; JiJi Foundation; Marty and Pamela Krasney; Robert and Karen Kustel, in honor of Bruce Kelley; Guy Lampard and Suzanne Badenhoop; LEF Foundation; Michael McCone; Moore Family Foundation; National Endowment for the Arts; National Park Service; David and Lucile Packard Foundation; Pease Family Fund, in honor of Bruce Kelley; PhotoWings; Resources Legacy Fund; Alan Rosenus; Rosie the Riveter/WWII Home Front NHP; The San Francisco Foundation; San Manuel Band of Mission Indians; Deborah Sanchez; Savory Thymes; Hans Schoepflin; Contee and Maggie Seely; James B. Swinerton; Swinerton Family Fund; Taproot Foundation; TomKat Charitable Trust; Lisa Van Cleef and Mark Gunson; Marion Weber; John Wiley & Sons; Peter Booth Wiley; and Yocha Dehe Wintun Nation.

Getting Involved

To learn more about our publications, events, membership club, and other ways you can participate, please visit www.heydaybooks.com.